ULTIMATE Bucket LIST

FOR MARRIED COUPLES

A COUPLE'S JOURNAL

FOR PLANNING YOUR
Best EXPERIENCES TOGETHER

ALEX DAVIS & RYAN GLEASON

Illustrated by Ella Lama

Zeitgeist • New York

Published in the United States by Zeitgeist, an imprint of Zeitgeist™,
a division of Penguin Random House LLC, New York.
penguinrandomhouse.com

Zeitgeist™ is a trademark of Penguin Random House LLC

ISBN: 9780593436080

Illustrations by Ella Lama
Book design by Erin Yeung
Edited by Kim Suarez

Printed in the United States of America

1 3 5 7 9 10 8 6 4 2

First Edition

I, _____, and I, _____,

take this bucket list to be our lifelong journey

toward happiness, love, and fulfillment.

To all of our grandparents—
your lives lived fully inspire us every day.

Li Li Hua, Yien Chuen, Wu Tsungyi,
Marion, and Robert; and Rose, Peggy, Dick,
LaVerne, and Thomas

Contents

Introduction 11

The Planner 14

Sample Bucket List Item 28

Notes 148

Acknowledgments 155

References 156

About the Authors 157

Your Bucket List Items

30	60
(Fill out completed bucket list item here)	
32	62
34	66
36	68
38	70
42	72
44	74
46	78
48	80
50	82
54	84
56	86
58	90

92

94

96

98

102

104

106

108

110

114

116

118

120

122

126

128

130

132

134

138

140

142

144

146

Introduction

*W*hen we met working as engineers in a laboratory—goofy safety goggles and all—we didn't know what adventures were in store for us. All we knew was that we each had met our match.

As we started dating, we took our engineering values of curiosity and experimentation with us everywhere we went. We wanted to become the healthiest and happiest couple we could be, even if that meant being guinea pigs in the process!

We figured the best way to hold ourselves accountable was to lead by example. So we became health coaches to help others reach their fitness and nutrition goals, and we documented everything we learned on our blog.

Soon we noticed a trend: the couples who worked out and cooked healthy meals together were the ones who succeeded in reaching their goals over the long term. As a newly married couple ourselves, we took note and expanded our research into the psychology and science of relationships.

Together, we were committed to a healthy lifestyle above all else. So it was a rude awakening when doctors diagnosed Ryan, husband and coauthor of this book, with severe burnout from work. To refocus on our well-being and fulfill a lifelong dream of living abroad, we quit our jobs and moved to South America.

With our new life came new passions and new goals. We had been so focused on our careers that we didn't have structured life aspirations or relationship goals. So, in a little leafy café in Ecuador, we wrote our first couple's bucket list.

What started as a bucket list of things we wanted to do in South America soon transformed into a road map of ambitions for all stages of life and marriage. We listed dreams for when we have kids and dreams for when we retire.

From lofty goals like running a marathon on every major continent to small aspirations like leaving a living legacy of bonsai trees, our couple's bucket list became the blueprint for building our relationship together and leaving our mark on the world.

Essentially, a bucket list is just that: a compilation of goals and dreams to live a fulfilling life. And it's more than just a to-do list. Building a couple's bucket list and sharing everything from your well-known ideas to your wildest dreams is an opportunity to connect meaningfully with your partner in a fun and natural way. This bucket list gives you a chance to evaluate where you are in life and visualize your future accomplishments, all while strengthening your relationship.

According to a popular study, writing down your goals, as you'll do in this guided journal, makes you 42 percent more likely to succeed. Additional research shows that having your partner as an accountability buddy makes you up to three times more likely to stick to a task.

For years we've harnessed the power of bucket lists within our marriage. Half the fun is simply talking about and laughing over our list of ideas while the other half is enjoying new experiences together (which, according to science, increases relationship satisfaction and makes you fall more in love).

In this book, we guide you step-by-step in choosing achievable goals that also challenge your limits. As engineers, we share science-backed strategies on how to make your couple's bucket list a reality.

No matter where you are in your life, relationship, or health, there is always space for more growth, laughter, and connection.

What's Inside

Part planner and part journal, this book encourages and guides you not only in dreaming up life-changing adventures, but also in bringing these dreams, desires, goals, and visions into existence.

The first section covers how to meaningfully brainstorm. Through guided questions, idea development, and fun and practical themes, you may discover some deep-rooted dreams and interests you didn't even know your partner had.

From there, fill in your bucket list journal entries to celebrate your journey. There is even enough space to add something special, like a photo , sticker, or ticket stub!

How to Use This Journal

Building the ultimate bucket list that's both personal and deeply meaningful takes thought and creativity. Use the foundational themes in this journal to discover the things most important to you as a couple. No matter how wild, record them on your worksheet.

Of course, factors like timing, family lifestyle, health, and budget will always play a role in the process. This is something we'll discuss in the Practical Planning section. We'll also ensure that your bucket list isn't simply a wish list but one that is achievable, exhilarating, and unique to you as a couple.

Last, use the Planning Tips and Solutions to navigate through common obstacles when creating a successful couple's bucket list.

Let's get started!

The Planner

*D*id you know that planning out and pursuing goals can boost happiness and satisfaction, even if they haven't yet been achieved?

As a married couple doing our best to lead a fulfilling life together, we know how rewarding and helpful it is to make a bucket list. Talking about lifelong dreams connects us on a deeper level, and we always learn something fun and new about each other. That's because as we grow, our dreams for ourselves and our marriage grow too.

Even if you and your loved one have different interests, limitations on your budget or time, or are simply at a different stage in your marriage, you can still create your dream list with thoughtful discussions and careful planning.

Bucket List Building

Building your bucket list isn't an exact science, but research shows that just the act of getting your goals written down provides a sense of relief and accomplishes the first step toward achieving them.

We recommend that you start by having a sincere discussion about the life experiences you want to have as a couple. Don't worry about crafting the "perfect" list, just one that gets you excited for the life you and your partner will lead. Your list, just like your relationship, can always evolve over time. And have fun with it!

To kick off bucket list building, we include nine foundational themes to craft a well-rounded bucket list and get the creative juices flowing.

Achievable and Practical Goals

Think about what you can accomplish within the next three months. If that feels too far out, just think about the next three weeks. These small goals may seem simple, but even the smallest changes can add value to your life. Rely on each other for accountability to accomplish these goals together while building momentum to tackle even more.

- Create a family budget
- Start a website or business page for your side gig
- Build a yoga, meditation, or art space in your home
- Host a dinner party using your best recipes
- Interview relatives to help build your family tree

Something That Scares You

Is there something you admire others for doing but never thought you could do yourselves? Or is there something that you feel compelled to do but are just too scared? Discomfort is an integral part of the growth process, so try to think of it as your own powerful tool. The opportunities you take to step out of your comfort zones are often the most fulfilling times of your lives.

- Temporarily move abroad
- Give a speech in front of a crowd of people
- Downsize your belongings and move into a tiny house
- Have one conversation with a stranger every day
- Ask for advice from someone you both look up to

Wellness Activities

Health is your greatest wealth, and the healthier you are, the more variety you can add to your bucket list. While health is a state of being, wellness is a state of living. Wellness has a direct influence on our health since it integrates our physical, mental, and spiritual well-being. Take some time to brainstorm a list of your biggest weekly stressors and your biggest weekly joys. Use those to build your bucket list's wellness ideas.

- ▷ Take an aerial or acrobatic yoga class
- ▷ Pick up a new hobby like rock climbing or painting
- ▷ Plant a garden and grow your own vegetables
- ▷ Start a neighborhood walking group
- ▷ Read all the classics together

Spiritual Learning

What does spirituality mean to you? To some, it may stem from religious beliefs, while for others, it may be linked to a more holistic or scientific quest for purpose and meaning. To us, spiritual learning is deeply personal, and it brings us closer to a sense of peace, purpose, and connection. How can you and your partner connect on a deeper, more spiritual level?

- ▷ Attend a couples retreat
- ▷ Hike a historical or cultural route you can connect to
- ▷ Take a meditation class
- ▷ Each choose to forgive an old enemy or let go of a heavy grudge
- ▷ Reflect and practice gratitude in a daily journal that can be passed back and forth

Mobility and Strength

Which ideas on your bucket list require the most strength and endurance? Or, outside of physical capability, which activities involve "roughing it"? A few items may become unattainable or less desirable as you age. Let's face it, attending a full weekend concert in the desert or sleeping in a tent in the wilderness might not sound so cool or fun as it did when you were twenty-four. Assess and prioritize what you should do sooner rather than later.

- Summit a mountain on a new continent
- Go backcountry camping, carrying everything you need in a backpack
- Do an obstacle course race
- Join a local bowling or flag football league
- Build a small cabin or tree house by hand

Seasonal Activities

Think of your favorite seasonal activities. Are there lifelong dreams that you want to accomplish? Work these ideas into your calendar and plan ahead. They only happen at special times!

- Catch the great wildebeest migration
- Take a dogsledding trip
- Attend a special event, like Carnival or the Olympics
- Stargaze under the northern lights
- Go on a fall foliage road trip

Must-See Places

Would you rather travel to a place with great history or phenomenal food? Do you prefer to travel to as many countries as possible or spend time in only one, living like a local? Are you on the same page regarding travel, or does one of you prefer to travel the world with a backpack while the other wants to return to the same resort yearly? Do your best to balance your ideas and create a combined list of must-see destinations.

- Visit an ancestor's hometown
- Sail along the Nile River
- Camp in every national park within your home country
- Plan a vacation around your favorite foods or beverages
- Swim in every ocean

Skills and Classes

Which skills could you learn (or relearn) to enhance other bucket list items? Or are there interests that you've never followed up on? Acquiring new skills to add to your repertoire, even if they don't seem relevant to other areas of your life, has been shown to boost happiness and feelings of purpose.

- Learn how to scuba dive
- Make every recipe in a cookbook
- Take music lessons
- Learn a new language
- Complete a wilderness survival course

Charitable Acts

Giving is the greatest gift of all. What gifts might you receive in return once you start donating your time, talents, or finances together? There are many ways to give back with charitable acts. They can be done locally or overseas, in person or online, and in small or big ways. Take time to think about which causes or organizations are really meaningful and unique to you as a couple.

- Become regular volunteers at a local spot
- Coach a sports team
- Help a family in need build a home
- Donate your professional skills to a nonprofit or charity
- Adopt a child (or at least a pet!)

Practical Planning

To experience something epic like those items in your bucket list, there has to be an element of practicality to your planning. Be realistic about your limitations (budget, number of vacation days, specific family needs, and so on) while also taking them as a challenge to get creative. Maybe you can't afford a trip to Iceland to see the northern lights, but they also shine bright in Minnesota. With careful planning, you can still build the ultimate bucket list.

Time Goals

As they say, timing is everything. For each item, think of when you want to accomplish it. Is it something you can do now? Or would it make more sense in the future?

As we mentioned, some items may make more sense to do while you're younger or while you have an opportune moment (such as being in between jobs or taking a sabbatical). Or perhaps it's better to wait. Just make sure to have an idea of when you want to accomplish it, or else you may end up never doing it.

Family Life

Crossing off your bucket list items works best when considering your family's needs and situation. What does your family look like right now, and how might that change in the future? Newlyweds and retired folks may have more freedom (and disposable income) than a family of six. Which bucket list items make sense to do sooner—and which ones later?

Budget

Don't let your dreams get pushed aside solely because of money. Since this is your ultimate bucket list, these are the most important and memorable things you'll do in a lifetime.

If you don't have enough savings or extra income to fulfill your bucket list today, figure out how much your goals will cost. Prioritize your big-ticket, must-have items and start structuring a budget to save up. Steadily put some money aside for these activities, and it will be the best money you've ever spent.

Planning Tips and Solutions

To ensure that your couple's bucket list doesn't remain simply a wish list, consider these planning tips and solutions to help you get started. Every couple has a unique situation, so discuss any limitations and start taking step-by-step actions to achieve your goals.

Keep an open mind when navigating differing interests. The beautiful thing about being in a couple is that you're different from each other. As we look back at our own couple's bucket list, it's evident just how many rewarding experiences we could have missed out on if we had only listed our mutual interests. While most items on your couple's bucket list should be things you're equally enthused about, it's important to support and celebrate your partner's passions. They might become shared, after all.

Commit now and think later. Many of your bucket list items may be long-term or challenging, but it's human nature to want to take the quick and easy route. So how do you manage this? Think of the first steps that can easily be taken to commit yourself to the goal. Whether that's reserving your spots in a marathon a year out, booking a flight, or publicly announcing your goal on social media, make sure to create a commitment device that will hold you accountable and start you on a path toward success.

Consolidate your list as much as possible to save time and money. If one of your goals is to go on safari in South Africa, what else on your list can be crossed off during the same trip? Diving with great white sharks? Surfing with penguins? It's a wonderful feeling to accomplish more than one goal at a time.

Read your bucket list together and often. Your bucket list shouldn't be a list you write and forget about. Like a living document, it will change and grow over time. Reading it often will help you find more opportunities to redefine and achieve your goals. Keep this bucket list journal somewhere you can both see it, like on a coffee table or nightstand. Or set a reminder on your calendar to review your couple's bucket list quarterly, like a performance review.

Plan in advance and save more money. For big trips, don't necessarily book an all-inclusive package with tour guides. Spend time researching, chatting with locals online, reading blog reviews, and making a custom, cost-effective itinerary. Keep your schedule flexible as well; you never know what insider tips your barista might share once you get there!

Remember that some of the best things in life are free. From a published poem to a mountain climbed, many of the most fulfilling things you can do together don't come with a sizable price tag. As you begin tackling your couple's bucket list, schedule in a mix of activities that rely more on your personal strengths and talents than the size of your wallets.

Don't feel like you can't do your big bucket list items with kids. When we started traveling full-time, everyone told us it was great to do "before we had kids." Since then, we have met families traveling with kids of all ages and realized it doesn't have to be a limitation. Think outside the box and take advantage of opportunities such as online schooling, traveling during the summer holidays, or finding a home swap or pet-sitting gig. While it may be more challenging traveling with children, with challenge comes more reward.

Invite another couple to join you for big trips and activities. Review your bucket list ideas and think of friends or family members with similar interests. You can start new traditions and save on group discounts!

BUCKET LIST BRAINSTORMING WORKSHEET

As you brainstorm your couple's bucket list, record your ideas on this worksheet. In addition to the nine foundational themes, there is space for you to come up with three more themes. Get creative, and remember, no idea is too wild!

ACHIEVABLE AND PRACTICAL GOALS

SOMETHING THAT SCARES YOU

WELLNESS ACTIVITIES

SPIRITUAL LEARNING

MOBILITY AND STRENGTH

SEASONAL ACTIVITIES

MUST-SEE PLACES

SKILLS AND CLASSES

CHARITABLE ACTS

(Fill in your own theme)

(Fill in your own theme)

(Fill in your own theme)

To accomplish great things, we must not only act, but also dream; not only plan, but also believe.

—ANATOLE FRANCE

SAMPLE BUCKET LIST ITEM

Backcountry Camping
FILL IN BUCKET LIST ITEM

WHERE Palo Duro Canyon State Park, Texas, USA

WHEN November 23-26, 2017

WHAT INSPIRED YOU TO DO THIS? It was a childhood dream of Ryan's to go into the wilderness, carrying everything you need in a backpack. Ryan grew up spending many nights at campsites, but never out in the backcountry where nothing is around but the stars.

STORIES AND ADVENTURES (i.e., describe the overall experience—what you were thinking, what you saw, who you met, any challenges you faced, weirdest thing that happened, scariest thing, and so on)

We had a phenomenal trip, and one that will inspire many more backcountry camping trips to come! It was tough, and at times freezing, but unforgettable until the end. There is something so empowering about being able to rely on your skills and live out in nature with no one else around, even if just for a few nights. Our favorite memory is cooking outside on our little stove while enjoying the sunsets and playing cards under our headlamps. The most hilarious memory is when a raccoon ran away with one of Ryan's shoes!

SOMETHING NEW YOU LEARNED ABOUT EACH OTHER

Ryan learned that Alex is really, really tough! She carried a lot of weight (literally and figuratively), never sweat, and never complained. Alex learned that Ryan is a fastidious and meticulous planner who will unpack and repack her backpack if it's not up to snuff. Also, he will not rest until he finds the perfect campsite! It's clear that Ryan loves taking care of Alex.

HOW HAS THIS BROUGHT YOU CLOSER?

Backcountry camping is the ultimate exercise in teamwork. Everyone has important roles, and the stakes are higher when you're in the middle of the wilderness. We needed to fully trust and rely on each other, and backcountry camping pushed us past our normal physical and mental limits. We're closer than ever and have a newfound respect for each other.

WHERE ....

WHEN ....

WHAT INSPIRED YOU TO DO THIS? ....

....

....

....

....

ADD MEMORIES HERE—
PASTE IN A PHOTO, TICKET STUB, OR
ANOTHER ITEM FROM YOUR TRIP!

STORIES AND ADVENTURES

SOMETHING NEW YOU LEARNED ABOUT EACH OTHER

HOW HAS THIS BROUGHT YOU CLOSER?

WHERE ....

WHEN ....

WHAT INSPIRED YOU TO DO THIS? ....

....

....

....

ADD MEMORIES HERE—
PASTE IN A PHOTO, TICKET STUB, OR
ANOTHER ITEM FROM YOUR TRIP!

STORIES AND ADVENTURES

SOMETHING NEW YOU LEARNED ABOUT EACH OTHER

HOW HAS THIS BROUGHT YOU CLOSER?

FILL IN BUCKET LIST ITEM

WHERE ....

WHEN ....

WHAT INSPIRED YOU TO DO THIS? ....

....

....

....

....

ADD MEMORIES HERE—
PASTE IN A PHOTO, TICKET STUB, OR
ANOTHER ITEM FROM YOUR TRIP!

STORIES AND ADVENTURES

SOMETHING NEW YOU LEARNED ABOUT EACH OTHER

HOW HAS THIS BROUGHT YOU CLOSER?

FILL IN BUCKET LIST ITEM

WHERE ....

WHEN ....

WHAT INSPIRED YOU TO DO THIS? ....

....

....

....

....

ADD MEMORIES HERE—
PASTE IN A PHOTO, TICKET STUB, OR
ANOTHER ITEM FROM YOUR TRIP!

STORIES AND ADVENTURES

SOMETHING NEW YOU LEARNED ABOUT EACH OTHER

HOW HAS THIS BROUGHT YOU CLOSER?

FILL IN BUCKET LIST ITEM

WHERE ....

WHEN ....

WHAT INSPIRED YOU TO DO THIS? ....

....

....

....

....

ADD MEMORIES HERE—
PASTE IN A PHOTO, TICKET STUB, OR
ANOTHER ITEM FROM YOUR TRIP!

STORIES AND ADVENTURES

SOMETHING NEW YOU LEARNED ABOUT EACH OTHER

HOW HAS THIS BROUGHT YOU CLOSER?

MY ACTIONS ARE MY ONLY TRUE BELONGINGS.

—THICH NHAT HANH

FILL IN BUCKET LIST ITEM

WHERE ....

WHEN ....

WHAT INSPIRED YOU TO DO THIS? ....

....

....

....

ADD MEMORIES HERE—
PASTE IN A PHOTO, TICKET STUB, OR
ANOTHER ITEM FROM YOUR TRIP!

STORIES AND ADVENTURES

SOMETHING NEW YOU LEARNED ABOUT EACH OTHER

HOW HAS THIS BROUGHT YOU CLOSER?

WHERE

WHEN

WHAT INSPIRED YOU TO DO THIS?

ADD MEMORIES HERE—
PASTE IN A PHOTO, TICKET STUB, OR
ANOTHER ITEM FROM YOUR TRIP!

STORIES AND ADVENTURES

SOMETHING NEW YOU LEARNED ABOUT EACH OTHER

HOW HAS THIS BROUGHT YOU CLOSER?

FILL IN BUCKET LIST ITEM

WHERE ....

WHEN ....

WHAT INSPIRED YOU TO DO THIS? ....

....

....

....

....

ADD MEMORIES HERE—
PASTE IN A PHOTO, TICKET STUB, OR
ANOTHER ITEM FROM YOUR TRIP!

STORIES AND ADVENTURES

SOMETHING NEW YOU LEARNED ABOUT EACH OTHER

HOW HAS THIS BROUGHT YOU CLOSER?

FILL IN BUCKET LIST ITEM

WHERE ....

WHEN ....

WHAT INSPIRED YOU TO DO THIS? ....

....

....

....

....

ADD MEMORIES HERE—
PASTE IN A PHOTO, TICKET STUB, OR
ANOTHER ITEM FROM YOUR TRIP!

STORIES AND ADVENTURES

SOMETHING NEW YOU LEARNED ABOUT EACH OTHER

HOW HAS THIS BROUGHT YOU CLOSER?

FILL IN BUCKET LIST ITEM

WHERE ....

WHEN ....

WHAT INSPIRED YOU TO DO THIS? ....

....

....

....

....

ADD MEMORIES HERE—
PASTE IN A PHOTO, TICKET STUB, OR
ANOTHER ITEM FROM YOUR TRIP!

STORIES AND ADVENTURES

SOMETHING NEW YOU LEARNED ABOUT EACH OTHER

HOW HAS THIS BROUGHT YOU CLOSER?

It is not true that people stop pursuing dreams because they grow old, they grow old because they stop pursuing dreams.

—GABRIEL GARCÍA MÁRQUEZ

WHERE

WHEN

WHAT INSPIRED YOU TO DO THIS?

ADD MEMORIES HERE—
PASTE IN A PHOTO, TICKET STUB, OR
ANOTHER ITEM FROM YOUR TRIP!

STORIES AND ADVENTURES

SOMETHING NEW YOU LEARNED ABOUT EACH OTHER

HOW HAS THIS BROUGHT YOU CLOSER?

WHERE

WHEN

WHAT INSPIRED YOU TO DO THIS?

ADD MEMORIES HERE—
PASTE IN A PHOTO, TICKET STUB, OR
ANOTHER ITEM FROM YOUR TRIP!

STORIES AND ADVENTURES

SOMETHING NEW YOU LEARNED ABOUT EACH OTHER

HOW HAS THIS BROUGHT YOU CLOSER?

WHERE

WHEN

WHAT INSPIRED YOU TO DO THIS?

ADD MEMORIES HERE—
PASTE IN A PHOTO, TICKET STUB, OR
ANOTHER ITEM FROM YOUR TRIP!

STORIES AND ADVENTURES

SOMETHING NEW YOU LEARNED ABOUT EACH OTHER

HOW HAS THIS BROUGHT YOU CLOSER?

FILL IN BUCKET LIST ITEM

WHERE

WHEN

WHAT INSPIRED YOU TO DO THIS?

ADD MEMORIES HERE—
PASTE IN A PHOTO, TICKET STUB, OR
ANOTHER ITEM FROM YOUR TRIP!

STORIES AND ADVENTURES

SOMETHING NEW YOU LEARNED ABOUT EACH OTHER

HOW HAS THIS BROUGHT YOU CLOSER?

FILL IN BUCKET LIST ITEM

WHERE

WHEN

WHAT INSPIRED YOU TO DO THIS?

ADD MEMORIES HERE—
PASTE IN A PHOTO, TICKET STUB, OR
ANOTHER ITEM FROM YOUR TRIP!

STORIES AND ADVENTURES

SOMETHING NEW YOU LEARNED ABOUT EACH OTHER

HOW HAS THIS BROUGHT YOU CLOSER?

Having the courage
to stand up and pursue
your dreams will give
you life's greatest
reward and life's
greatest adventure.

—OPRAH WINFREY

WHERE

WHEN

WHAT INSPIRED YOU TO DO THIS?

ADD MEMORIES HERE—
PASTE IN A PHOTO, TICKET STUB, OR
ANOTHER ITEM FROM YOUR TRIP!

STORIES AND ADVENTURES

SOMETHING NEW YOU LEARNED ABOUT EACH OTHER

HOW HAS THIS BROUGHT YOU CLOSER?

WHERE

WHEN

WHAT INSPIRED YOU TO DO THIS?

ADD MEMORIES HERE—
PASTE IN A PHOTO, TICKET STUB, OR
ANOTHER ITEM FROM YOUR TRIP!

STORIES AND ADVENTURES

SOMETHING NEW YOU LEARNED ABOUT EACH OTHER

HOW HAS THIS BROUGHT YOU CLOSER?

FILL IN BUCKET LIST ITEM

WHERE ....

WHEN ....

WHAT INSPIRED YOU TO DO THIS? ....

....

....

....

....

ADD MEMORIES HERE—
PASTE IN A PHOTO, TICKET STUB, OR
ANOTHER ITEM FROM YOUR TRIP!

STORIES AND ADVENTURES

SOMETHING NEW YOU LEARNED ABOUT EACH OTHER

HOW HAS THIS BROUGHT YOU CLOSER?

FILL IN BUCKET LIST ITEM

WHERE

WHEN

WHAT INSPIRED YOU TO DO THIS?

ADD MEMORIES HERE—
PASTE IN A PHOTO, TICKET STUB, OR
ANOTHER ITEM FROM YOUR TRIP!

STORIES AND ADVENTURES

SOMETHING NEW YOU LEARNED ABOUT EACH OTHER

HOW HAS THIS BROUGHT YOU CLOSER?

WHERE ....

WHEN ....

WHAT INSPIRED YOU TO DO THIS? ....

....

....

....

....

ADD MEMORIES HERE—
PASTE IN A PHOTO, TICKET STUB, OR
ANOTHER ITEM FROM YOUR TRIP!

STORIES AND ADVENTURES

SOMETHING NEW YOU LEARNED ABOUT EACH OTHER

HOW HAS THIS BROUGHT YOU CLOSER?

The more one does and sees and feels, the more one is able to do, and the more genuine may be one's appreciation of fundamental things like home, and love, and understanding companionship.

−AMELIA EARHART

FILL IN BUCKET LIST ITEM

WHERE ....

WHEN ....

WHAT INSPIRED YOU TO DO THIS? ....

....

....

....

....

ADD MEMORIES HERE—
PASTE IN A PHOTO, TICKET STUB, OR
ANOTHER ITEM FROM YOUR TRIP!

STORIES AND ADVENTURES

SOMETHING NEW YOU LEARNED ABOUT EACH OTHER

HOW HAS THIS BROUGHT YOU CLOSER?

FILL IN BUCKET LIST ITEM

WHERE ....

WHEN ....

WHAT INSPIRED YOU TO DO THIS? ....

....

....

....

....

ADD MEMORIES HERE—
PASTE IN A PHOTO, TICKET STUB, OR
ANOTHER ITEM FROM YOUR TRIP!

STORIES AND ADVENTURES

SOMETHING NEW YOU LEARNED ABOUT EACH OTHER

HOW HAS THIS BROUGHT YOU CLOSER?

WHERE

WHEN

WHAT INSPIRED YOU TO DO THIS?

ADD MEMORIES HERE—
PASTE IN A PHOTO, TICKET STUB, OR
ANOTHER ITEM FROM YOUR TRIP!

STORIES AND ADVENTURES

SOMETHING NEW YOU LEARNED ABOUT EACH OTHER

HOW HAS THIS BROUGHT YOU CLOSER?

WHERE

WHEN

WHAT INSPIRED YOU TO DO THIS?

ADD MEMORIES HERE—
PASTE IN A PHOTO, TICKET STUB, OR
ANOTHER ITEM FROM YOUR TRIP!

STORIES AND ADVENTURES

SOMETHING NEW YOU LEARNED ABOUT EACH OTHER

HOW HAS THIS BROUGHT YOU CLOSER?

WHERE ....

WHEN ....

WHAT INSPIRED YOU TO DO THIS? ....

....

....

....

....

ADD MEMORIES HERE—
PASTE IN A PHOTO, TICKET STUB, OR
ANOTHER ITEM FROM YOUR TRIP!

STORIES AND ADVENTURES

SOMETHING NEW YOU LEARNED ABOUT EACH OTHER

HOW HAS THIS BROUGHT YOU CLOSER?

YOU ARE NEVER TOO OLD TO SET ANOTHER GOAL OR TO DREAM A NEW DREAM.

—LES BROWN

WHERE ....

WHEN ....

WHAT INSPIRED YOU TO DO THIS? ....

....

....

....

....

ADD MEMORIES HERE—
PASTE IN A PHOTO, TICKET STUB, OR
ANOTHER ITEM FROM YOUR TRIP!

STORIES AND ADVENTURES

SOMETHING NEW YOU LEARNED ABOUT EACH OTHER

HOW HAS THIS BROUGHT YOU CLOSER?

WHERE

WHEN

WHAT INSPIRED YOU TO DO THIS?

ADD MEMORIES HERE—
PASTE IN A PHOTO, TICKET STUB, OR
ANOTHER ITEM FROM YOUR TRIP!

STORIES AND ADVENTURES

SOMETHING NEW YOU LEARNED ABOUT EACH OTHER

HOW HAS THIS BROUGHT YOU CLOSER?

WHERE

WHEN

WHAT INSPIRED YOU TO DO THIS?

ADD MEMORIES HERE—
PASTE IN A PHOTO, TICKET STUB, OR
ANOTHER ITEM FROM YOUR TRIP!

STORIES AND ADVENTURES

SOMETHING NEW YOU LEARNED ABOUT EACH OTHER

HOW HAS THIS BROUGHT YOU CLOSER?

WHERE

WHEN

WHAT INSPIRED YOU TO DO THIS?

ADD MEMORIES HERE—
PASTE IN A PHOTO, TICKET STUB, OR
ANOTHER ITEM FROM YOUR TRIP!

STORIES AND ADVENTURES

SOMETHING NEW YOU LEARNED ABOUT EACH OTHER

HOW HAS THIS BROUGHT YOU CLOSER?

WHERE

WHEN

WHAT INSPIRED YOU TO DO THIS?

ADD MEMORIES HERE—
PASTE IN A PHOTO, TICKET STUB, OR
ANOTHER ITEM FROM YOUR TRIP!

STORIES AND ADVENTURES

SOMETHING NEW YOU LEARNED ABOUT EACH OTHER

HOW HAS THIS BROUGHT YOU CLOSER?

FILL YOUR LIFE WITH TINY AND LARGE ADVENTUROUS MOMENTS.

—SARK

FILL IN BUCKET LIST ITEM

WHERE ....

WHEN ....

WHAT INSPIRED YOU TO DO THIS? ....

....

....

....

....

ADD MEMORIES HERE—
PASTE IN A PHOTO, TICKET STUB, OR
ANOTHER ITEM FROM YOUR TRIP!

STORIES AND ADVENTURES

SOMETHING NEW YOU LEARNED ABOUT EACH OTHER

HOW HAS THIS BROUGHT YOU CLOSER?

WHERE

WHEN

WHAT INSPIRED YOU TO DO THIS?

ADD MEMORIES HERE—
PASTE IN A PHOTO, TICKET STUB, OR
ANOTHER ITEM FROM YOUR TRIP!

STORIES AND ADVENTURES

SOMETHING NEW YOU LEARNED ABOUT EACH OTHER

HOW HAS THIS BROUGHT YOU CLOSER?

WHERE

WHEN

WHAT INSPIRED YOU TO DO THIS?

ADD MEMORIES HERE—
PASTE IN A PHOTO, TICKET STUB, OR
ANOTHER ITEM FROM YOUR TRIP!

STORIES AND ADVENTURES

SOMETHING NEW YOU LEARNED ABOUT EACH OTHER

HOW HAS THIS BROUGHT YOU CLOSER?

WHERE

WHEN

WHAT INSPIRED YOU TO DO THIS?

ADD MEMORIES HERE—
PASTE IN A PHOTO, TICKET STUB, OR
ANOTHER ITEM FROM YOUR TRIP!

STORIES AND ADVENTURES

SOMETHING NEW YOU LEARNED ABOUT EACH OTHER

HOW HAS THIS BROUGHT YOU CLOSER?

FILL IN BUCKET LIST ITEM

WHERE

WHEN

WHAT INSPIRED YOU TO DO THIS?

ADD MEMORIES HERE—
PASTE IN A PHOTO, TICKET STUB, OR
ANOTHER ITEM FROM YOUR TRIP!

STORIES AND ADVENTURES

SOMETHING NEW YOU LEARNED ABOUT EACH OTHER

HOW HAS THIS BROUGHT YOU CLOSER?

ALL LIFE IS AN
EXPERIMENT. THE
MORE EXPERIMENTS
YOU MAKE THE
BETTER.

—RALPH WALDO EMERSON

FILL IN BUCKET LIST ITEM

WHERE

WHEN

WHAT INSPIRED YOU TO DO THIS?

ADD MEMORIES HERE—
PASTE IN A PHOTO, TICKET STUB, OR
ANOTHER ITEM FROM YOUR TRIP!

STORIES AND ADVENTURES

SOMETHING NEW YOU LEARNED ABOUT EACH OTHER

HOW HAS THIS BROUGHT YOU CLOSER?

FILL IN BUCKET LIST ITEM

WHERE ....

WHEN ....

WHAT INSPIRED YOU TO DO THIS? ....

....

....

....

....

ADD MEMORIES HERE—
PASTE IN A PHOTO, TICKET STUB, OR
ANOTHER ITEM FROM YOUR TRIP!

STORIES AND ADVENTURES

SOMETHING NEW YOU LEARNED ABOUT EACH OTHER

HOW HAS THIS BROUGHT YOU CLOSER?

WHERE ....

WHEN ....

WHAT INSPIRED YOU TO DO THIS? ....

....

....

....

....

ADD MEMORIES HERE—
PASTE IN A PHOTO, TICKET STUB, OR
ANOTHER ITEM FROM YOUR TRIP!

STORIES AND ADVENTURES

SOMETHING NEW YOU LEARNED ABOUT EACH OTHER

HOW HAS THIS BROUGHT YOU CLOSER?

WHERE ....

WHEN ....

WHAT INSPIRED YOU TO DO THIS? ....

....

....

....

....

ADD MEMORIES HERE—
PASTE IN A PHOTO, TICKET STUB, OR
ANOTHER ITEM FROM YOUR TRIP!

STORIES AND ADVENTURES

SOMETHING NEW YOU LEARNED ABOUT EACH OTHER

HOW HAS THIS BROUGHT YOU CLOSER?

WHERE

WHEN

WHAT INSPIRED YOU TO DO THIS?

ADD MEMORIES HERE—
PASTE IN A PHOTO, TICKET STUB, OR
ANOTHER ITEM FROM YOUR TRIP!

STORIES AND ADVENTURES

SOMETHING NEW YOU LEARNED ABOUT EACH OTHER

HOW HAS THIS BROUGHT YOU CLOSER?

To live is to experience things, not sit around pondering the meaning of life.

—PAULO COELHO

WHERE

WHEN

WHAT INSPIRED YOU TO DO THIS?

ADD MEMORIES HERE—
PASTE IN A PHOTO, TICKET STUB, OR
ANOTHER ITEM FROM YOUR TRIP!

STORIES AND ADVENTURES

SOMETHING NEW YOU LEARNED ABOUT EACH OTHER

HOW HAS THIS BROUGHT YOU CLOSER?

WHERE

WHEN

WHAT INSPIRED YOU TO DO THIS?

ADD MEMORIES HERE—
PASTE IN A PHOTO, TICKET STUB, OR
ANOTHER ITEM FROM YOUR TRIP!

STORIES AND ADVENTURES

SOMETHING NEW YOU LEARNED ABOUT EACH OTHER

HOW HAS THIS BROUGHT YOU CLOSER?

FILL IN BUCKET LIST ITEM

WHERE

WHEN

WHAT INSPIRED YOU TO DO THIS?

ADD MEMORIES HERE—
PASTE IN A PHOTO, TICKET STUB, OR
ANOTHER ITEM FROM YOUR TRIP!

STORIES AND ADVENTURES

SOMETHING NEW YOU LEARNED ABOUT EACH OTHER

HOW HAS THIS BROUGHT YOU CLOSER?

WHERE

WHEN

WHAT INSPIRED YOU TO DO THIS?

ADD MEMORIES HERE—
PASTE IN A PHOTO, TICKET STUB, OR
ANOTHER ITEM FROM YOUR TRIP!

STORIES AND ADVENTURES

SOMETHING NEW YOU LEARNED ABOUT EACH OTHER

HOW HAS THIS BROUGHT YOU CLOSER?

FILL IN BUCKET LIST ITEM

WHERE

WHEN

WHAT INSPIRED YOU TO DO THIS?

ADD MEMORIES HERE—
PASTE IN A PHOTO, TICKET STUB, OR
ANOTHER ITEM FROM YOUR TRIP!

STORIES AND ADVENTURES

SOMETHING NEW YOU LEARNED ABOUT EACH OTHER

HOW HAS THIS BROUGHT YOU CLOSER?

If we did all the things we are capable of doing, we would literally astound ourselves.

—THOMAS EDISON

WHERE

WHEN

WHAT INSPIRED YOU TO DO THIS?

ADD MEMORIES HERE—
PASTE IN A PHOTO, TICKET STUB, OR
ANOTHER ITEM FROM YOUR TRIP!

STORIES AND ADVENTURES

SOMETHING NEW YOU LEARNED ABOUT EACH OTHER

HOW HAS THIS BROUGHT YOU CLOSER?

WHERE

WHEN

WHAT INSPIRED YOU TO DO THIS?

ADD MEMORIES HERE—
PASTE IN A PHOTO, TICKET STUB, OR
ANOTHER ITEM FROM YOUR TRIP!

STORIES AND ADVENTURES

SOMETHING NEW YOU LEARNED ABOUT EACH OTHER

HOW HAS THIS BROUGHT YOU CLOSER?

WHERE

WHEN

WHAT INSPIRED YOU TO DO THIS?

ADD MEMORIES HERE—
PASTE IN A PHOTO, TICKET STUB, OR
ANOTHER ITEM FROM YOUR TRIP!

STORIES AND ADVENTURES

SOMETHING NEW YOU LEARNED ABOUT EACH OTHER

HOW HAS THIS BROUGHT YOU CLOSER?

FILL IN BUCKET LIST ITEM

WHERE

WHEN

WHAT INSPIRED YOU TO DO THIS?

ADD MEMORIES HERE—
PASTE IN A PHOTO, TICKET STUB, OR
ANOTHER ITEM FROM YOUR TRIP!

STORIES AND ADVENTURES

SOMETHING NEW YOU LEARNED ABOUT EACH OTHER

HOW HAS THIS BROUGHT YOU CLOSER?

FILL IN BUCKET LIST ITEM

WHERE ....

WHEN ....

WHAT INSPIRED YOU TO DO THIS? ....

....

....

....

....

ADD MEMORIES HERE—
PASTE IN A PHOTO, TICKET STUB, OR
ANOTHER ITEM FROM YOUR TRIP!

STORIES AND ADVENTURES

SOMETHING NEW YOU LEARNED ABOUT EACH OTHER

HOW HAS THIS BROUGHT YOU CLOSER?

Notes

Acknowledgments

Writing this book together has been a deeply rewarding and fun experience. We couldn't have done it without the guidance of so many. Without their support, we would never have been brave enough to take the first steps in getting our dreams off the ground.

To Alex's parents, Teresa Yien and Randall Davis, for their unconditional love, wisdom, and endless opportunity. They didn't balk (too much) when we announced we were leaving our engineering jobs and cushy lives behind. Instead, they emboldened Alex with her new, favorite motto: Do one thing every day that scares your family.

To Ryan's parents, Julie and Patrick Gleason. Their guidance is legendary. Thank you for instilling in Ryan his creativity, sense of adventure, and love of family. He was so fortunate to learn from the best.

To Alex's sister, Anita Davis, and Ryan's sisters, Christine Lee and Anna Gleason. No one is as inspiring as a strong woman, and we have three magnificent women to look up to.

To our mentor, Ellen Malloy, who not only believed in two dreamers but helped us craft a plan to make our dreams a reality.

Finally, writing this book while in the first trimester of pregnancy with our first child was a challenge but a pure joy. Thank you, future son or daughter, for giving us perspective and reminding us what the important things are in life—and for expanding our bucket list with a whole new world of aspirations.

References

Gardner, Sarah and Dave Albee, "Study Focuses on Strategies for Achieving Goals, Resolutions." Dominican University of California, Feb. 1, 2015. Press release. 266.

Goldstein, Noah J. et al. *Yes!: 50 Scientifically Proven Ways to Be Persuasive*. New York: Free Press, 2010.

Aron, A. et al. "Couples' Shared Participation in Novel and Arousing Activities and Experienced Relationship Auality." *Journal of Personality and Social Psychology* 78 (2000): 273–84. doi:10.1037//0022-3514.78.2.273.

Nawijn, Jeroen et al. "Vacationers Happier, but Most Not Happier After a Holiday." *Applied Research in Quality of Life* 5 (2010): 35–47. doi:10.1007/s11482-009-9091-9.

About the Authors

 **Alex Davis** and **Ryan Gleason** are a husband-and-wife duo who empower couples to optimize their relationship, health, and well-being.

After graduating from different universities with the same engineering degree, Alex and Ryan met in a research laboratory, where they bonded over their love of white lab coats, unique experiences, and yearning to live an unconventional life.

Following eight years working internationally as corporate engineers, Alex and Ryan left their high-powered jobs to tackle their true passion—learning how to engineer the healthiest, happiest, and most fulfilling life possible. From this, the couple grew and launched ryanandalex.com with the mission to strengthen relationships and health through science, self-experimentation, and structured plans of action.

Alex is originally from Boston, Massachusetts, and Ryan hails from St. Paul, Minnesota. They now reside in Medellín, Colombia, with their growing family.

Visit ryanandalex.com to find out more.

Hi there,

We hope you enjoyed using *Ultimate Bucket List for Married Couples*. If you have any questions or concerns about your book, or have received a damaged copy, please contact customerservice@penguinrandomhouse.com. We're here and happy to help.

Also, please consider writing a review on your favorite retailer's website to let others know what you thought of the book!

Sincerely,
The Zeitgeist Team